Ryerson

NEW AND SELECTED POEMS

NEW AND SELECTED POEMS
1943-1985

ALICE RYERSON

SPOON RIVER POETRY PRESS
1987

This book is published in part with funds provided by the Illinois Arts Council, a state organization, and by the National Endowment for the Arts. Our thanks.

Published by Spoon River Poetry Press, David Pichaske, editor; P. O. Box 1443; Peoria, Illinois 61655.
Typesetting by Rodine the Printer, Peoria, Illinois.
Printing by M & D Printers, Henry, Illinois.
ISBN: 0-933180-98-5

"A mouse is miracle enough to stagger sextillions
of infidels."
                                    —Walt Whitman

CONTENTS

For Albert

A SEQUENCE OF BIRDS

Warblers

We stand by a clump of hawthorn
spangled with warblers.
Ninnies of happiness
we warble along in syncopated spring time.
Bobble your head and grin
at the flickering trinkets
the tininess of wings
perched on my ears
like sweet tickling wishes.

Great Blue Heron

It is August and you are predicting the heron.
The children keep watch on the pond.
Just before supper he crosses
low near the water between two dunes,
his chest puffed out like the prow of a ship,
legs streaming. Our reliable heron.
We all run down to the shore in bare feet
nestle into the sand
under those great laborious wings.

Gull

Dripping out of the hurricane
comes a stranger holding a gentle box.
"I wouldn't have bothered you
if it wasn't for this bird I found."
You and the stranger
consider together, looking in
at the fierce eye of terror
on a nest of folded rags.
The wind addles my brain
and I boil needless water.

Crow

Jerkily ceremonial, a crow
stalks the rim of the burnt out fire
blackening his heart with charcoal.
We are avoiding the embers, poking in the ashes.
What's burnt up? What's to be found?
Molten bottles twisted into omens?
Little black bones to toss like dice?
The crow caws away over the prairie
carrying something in his beak.

Pterodactyl

With a roar of feathers
ten feet of shadow goes over.
Will it plunge down the wind
onto some moment we care about?
We spread out wing-wide fingers
over our juicy children
as the pterodactyl
creaks bonily across the museum sky.

Goose and Hawk

Crossing this empty Sunday
we pass a wild goose
roosting on a kerb by a bus stop.
Now that you are going away
I'm not in the right place either.
Stumbling along the station platform
I look up to see a hobo hawk
riding awkwardly away
on the roof of your train.

I

BEYOND THE CANDLE

Beyond the candle, with one eye
    I watch your silence,
Perplexed and wondering that I,
    except by guessing,
Can never find the reason why
    your eyes are thinking,
However often I might buy
    thoughts with my pennies.

THE GREEN DRAGON

At dusk it flew
over the sweet-smelling bay,
shrank and grew
with the lilt of the wind.

The gulls spied,
curious and ill at ease
seeing it dive
when the breeze lagged.

We stood, stilled,
with our feet in brambles,
our bodies filled
with the zing of the held string.

Or were led through the wind
over boulders and blueberry
stumbling behind,
forgetting our feet to look up

Then as the night fell
we knotted, high on the string,
a small brass bell
and let the Green Dragon soar.

Bell-chiseled, soon
mysterious soft crystals
out of the moon
settled among the pasture rocks.

And in a hush
of blown glass silence,
under a bramble bush
the white moths bloomed.

The sand pricked hill
grew curly with the fluted roofs
of temples, still
and ancient among the baby juniper.

Down the string slant,
half the night, as the kite swung,
slid the clear chant
tinkling over the rough land.

FOG

Journals in crackling brown coats
clutter the summer mail
like katydids in August grass
calling in small insistent voices
little antiphonal messages from fate:
      Doom is. Doom isn't. Doom is. Doom isn't.
The sun has a louder voice,
wind, sea and rain shout down the chirping print
but in the fog it's amplified.

Wisps of fog bear me away
among the loud twittering.
The crackle of paper wrappings
explodes in every corner of the air
leaving a limbo of despair.
      Summer is only a paper house in the rain
      laced with sudden spiders descending.

When, crack! A mallet hits a ball
and all the warning of crickets
flickers out. Or nearly all.
Among the wickets
I see, with startled joy
a whole undamaged summer boy
taking his turn in the fog.
Gloom, thinned and lifted, blown away,
unveils the cheerful whacking of croquet.

A WOMAN IS A MARCH RIVER

She begins to melt.
A rivulet trickles down her breastbone
spreading into sunwarmed puddles.
Layers of cold are crumpling
as she uncurls towards a warm sky.
She is fluid again,
her veins thrum with dissolving crystals.
Hungry from hibernation
she gathers herself.

When she has stretched and thawed
you must run for the sandbags,
this is a river in old age
who has worn away all her meanders.
There will be cruel flashes of April,
drownings, houses torn apart,
and men sitting on rafters
careening down torrents.

But now she is March-slow
in the unfolding of water.

MATRIMONIAL PICNIC

All wound up
tin cans in tow
we tootle the highway
caution exit the cloverleaf
round the mulberry bush
to tin lizzy byways.
Mind the sign that says "bump."
Thimble tumble rumble bumble
over the wooden bridge
to the tootle ti root curve
where brown eyed cows
lope to the hoardings
to ogle our how now
leap over the ditch.
Will the raw tires take it?
Somebody's higgledy piggledy forest
crowds the ruts
at the next bend
thick to boggle even a logger
lover our axe may be ratchety
but the axles hold
as we jeep along beep along
out of the woods and away
from grandmother's house.
No wolves on *our* tail, tirra lirra
we trip the rattle and clap the trap
four cylinders and a squeaky toot
to the edge of the map
where deer jackers
peek from duck blinds.
While still ticking and tocking
from a well-wound start
we hippety hoppety
over the wagon ruts
into the at last meadow.

Out now honeys and bask
those juggled bundles of bones.
Here's a femur
so reach us the wrench
from the tool kit.
Is this your coccyx or mine
rattling on the floor boards?
But it doesn't really matter
because scrambled like eggs
we're the rambling gambling arrivers
at Here and Now.

IN BED

Discontinuous we lie
with an old cat asleep
between our backs

where jealous children
used to squirm
wedged in between us.

We grow old, you and I,
to be so equable, lying
back to cat and cat to back.

REMORSE

Eve
sorry
after the apple

knits
Adam
a softer figleaf

THE DEATH WATCHERS

This is a room
with a death happening in it,
thin and patient.
Women who have kept vigil
before ours
would recognize it:
the smell of fever and fear
and the curtains blowing fitfully.
Everything here has an old pattern.

He pushes covers slowly back
to cross his legs. They're hot
but crossing them to cool
is walking in deep sand.
He's folded up most of his life
and stacked it angrily
in other people's files
but the shreds he's kept
will be enough to die with.
It takes only the energy of one last breath
to finish the job.
He makes each necessary effort
conscientiously
dying his death himself
alone
with those who wait.

Sounds from the wet street
interrupt all night, as
past watchers sit in our minds
and tick like clocks.

OUT OF REACH

Beside the telephone
sits the repairman
studying the plug
alone

inside the wall
electricity cheeps
like mice

WOOLGATHERERS

The slow sheep group and regroup
like woolly molecules under a microscope
moving over the safe and drowsy grazing places.
Inedible reeds and rushes near water
rustle over the cool places where they sleep.
Beyond the cove called "Lovey's"
surf booms on the ocean beaches.
Our curiosity was lackadaisical with summer.
We lived here a long time
before we learned the sudden shocking news
that Lovey was a midget woolgatherer,

      one of a pair of tiny twins
      who threaded the sheep paths
      circumnavigated the bayberry and crept tired
      into the sleeping places of sheep
      where the twigs smelled of lanolin and roses
      and blackberries dropped into their mouths.

      With sacks slung over their shoulders,
      lunch in the pockets of their aprons,
      these child-sized women
      gathered the woolen tufts
      combed from the sheep by brambles.
      Miniature daughters of tall New Englanders
      they earned their way with these snippets of thrift.

      Little Lovey Mayhew and her nameless sister
      rested in the pasture as the tide came in.
      Late in the afternoon they crossed the creek
      wading through the shallows, both bags full.

      The summer moon deepened the pools
      in the swirling channel,
      the neap tide swept in and one small twin
      dragged down by the weight of her wet wool bundle,
      stumbled and drowned.

The full moon rises pale and early
as we stand in the groping eelgrass.
While the water rises around us
we woolgather at the far rim of summer.

AUTUMN DUSK

All day the millionaire sun beamed
on gold leaves in the garden,
the day had silver spoons in its mouth.
Now a late wind is gnawing the branches clean
exposing the travels of squirrels,
the interior life of trees.
A copper plate sky inked with branches
fades and goes out suddenly.

In the yard full of darkening
a jay shrieks a message
which the clear air makes clearer.
Tonight frost will bite
the six unpicked tomatoes.

II

EXPLORATION

The scrub growing outside my house
has thorny familiar blossoms.
It stretches into the sand on all sides
where the sand goes on to the horizon.
Now that I grow older I can explore that desert.
I throw a few things into a satchel,
untie my feet, and begin to walk.

The desert is full of brown until evening.
I am surprised at the low sun's intensity in the dry air.
I pass a shepherd weaving on a backstrap loom.
I scan his pattern as we pass:
palm leaves, jackals and fishes
on a wavy blue. His sheep are not with him
because there is nothing here to eat.

I pass through the clean centers of seven temples,
come to a prophet
standing at the wind blown blade of a dune.
He wears the shepherd's pattern.
We speak to each other
in pantomime.
We exchange ritual gifts,
figs for a chosen stone.

The first mirage is quite conventional,
palms, camels, woman-by-a-well.
The second is more personal: my own house
with a sphinx in the doorway.
The third is a shimmer on the desert sand.

Beyond these I come to the oasis,
footsore of course, and of course weary.
I drink and lie down
as one is expected to do in these places.
In the morning I will show my sand-blasted face
to whatever god presides over the place.

NEAR THE GREEN LEOPARD SEA

I am asleep walking
in a festival of lizard tracks.
Asleep walking to the end of the path
where the water waits booming
under the coral ledges.

This early it is my water.
Later when I have been washed down
to the size of awake
I will give it back to the fish.

THE TIBETAN

It's a good Saturday. I'll walk
to the theological seminary
to hear this Buddhist teacher talk.
I'm curious but also wary

of his still, puzzling smile;
Buddhas in museums don't lecture.
But this one after a while
begins to talk with a picture.

"A Zen poet," he says, with a pause,
"is a tree and a rock. And you see
this is very funny because
when the poet bends down the tree

over the rock, a frog hops through.
This makes the poet laugh
because, of course, he is the frog too."
The teacher chuckles and drinks half

a mug of saki on one of the tables.
Now what should I make of these
abstract toys and tangible fables
of the smiling man who is really trees?

GREEK MOUNTAINS

The mountains casually thrown
over the golden bones of the earth
lie rumpled and threadbare.

Their valleys run out of them
like honey draining into the plain.
They are bled lazy above their deltas.

Patched and darned with vineyards
they are laced together
with paths for the neat feet of donkeys.

They are used by old women
waist-deep in bobbing horns
leading their goats into basins of grass.

English ladies, with beaks extended
like gentle cranes,
botanize at their bases, while

those careful antiquarians, the cyclamen,
nibble away at the rock,
opening mouths in the mountain.

And out of these mouths
pour the words, the stones,
the golden bones themselves.

CHILDREN TO DISNEYLAND

Back home in Lowell
big brothers and sisters spent the day in school.
No one knew we were snowbound in Boston.

We waited twenty-four hours.
The loudspeaker of hope
came on with promises every half hour.
But every hour—as the snow softly continued—
the promises had to be broken.

We roosted all night
under the impassable air
whispering into each other's sleep
confident of the wonders waiting in Florida.

But in the morning our teacher telephoned the agency.
Still, nobody gave up hope
until the bus pulled up at the terminal
to take us through the yellow snow plows
back to Lowell.

The snow came down for three days on Boston
without stopping.
In Lowell too it snowed and snowed
in that winter of our disappointment.

SAND GARDEN

Streets spicy with sand
bask in the desert among calls
of dogs barking hunger.
Tapping feet pass early
on their way to an old religion.
Carefully take my hand
against this sea of worn walls.

Words, here in the dry mountains,
under the great iwans, are bird-light.
The courtyards fill with pilgrims
washing in cool pools
where water is precious as touch
and we slowly skirt the fountains
at the dry rim of night.

Dust and sleep ride on this bus
past where a praying shepherd kneels.
At our shoulders we can feel
the flimsy touch of sleeve on sleeve
as the bus swerves to avoid
the camel supercilious
drily eying these wheels.

Here rare trees overleaf
water, to make a stopping place.
The goatskin sacks lie like entrails
at the edge of the river
last water before love
is dammed into a reservoir of grief.
We cast ourselves like children into space.

The pointed arches are light, the tiles
draw arabesques across the sands.
Tired from noon climbing
we lean against white plaster in the shade.
Filtered wind plays us like fiddles . . .
I write you this after a thousand miles,
brushing the bright sand off my shoes and hands.

GUIDEBOOK

Shall we go north from Isfahan to Kermansha
on the road that is not recommended?
The nomads are out and moving in the desert
and if we want to keep dust in our shoes
it's the way we should go.

Probably the Persian miniatures we bought in Isfahan
would waste space in our light luggage
so we'll cache them for later.
You have a map and I trust you to find the way.

If we're lucky we'll find a guide with donkeys
and you can ride beside him
and ask questions in Farsi.
From time to time there's sure to be water.

If we make it across we can rent a car
to go back for our pictures
on the road recommended in the guidebook.

ARE YOU TRAPPED IN A RUSTY STEREOTYPE?

The trouble with getting old is
you can't say how shitty it is,
it shocks the young
who think you don't belong with words like that
because you keep the floors clean
make the beds and care about the view
(if not, they say "She's cracking up!").

So stand there. One foot in and one foot out.
Speak out of both sides of your old mouth.
"Oh fiddlesticks!" you say. "Fuck them!"

You potter through your tidy house
wearing your outer-directed bourgeois apron.
You wave your rolling pin, hum "Tea for Two"
while longing inside for an ashram.

It's hard to learn after fifty not to care
if the pictures hang straight on the walls,
learn not to water plants
or people.

Let 'em go, sister,
off to be happy monks
while you learn to sit
on a made bed
inviting what's left of your soul.

III

THE VISIT

1.

He has been there a month
when she comes with a thin bag
packed with nothing
that could expect anything in particular.
She didn't bring a face:
the people there will arrange one for her.

She has combed her words:
'These trees are beautiful.'
But what position should she stand in
to say so?

She looks at him sideways.
Anxiety closes her like a stopper.

2.

They eat a meal in easy postures
at a round table.
They pass the soup and crackers
but don't give out new faces yet.
He's laughing
with his chair tipped back.
She tosses on the surface
like a cork unable to dissolve.

3.

They climb through fields of stubble.
She crosses leafy places quietly
breathes as softly as she can
on an uphill path
because she's turning into an antenna,
listening.
Stopping to pick up apples
she catches her unquiet breath.

Is she tuned in to anything?
She thinks their silence
makes a minute rushing sound of its own.

4

Pretending great busyness
she nonchalantly wanders to her room
to fiddle with comfort:
too cold   too hot
she adds and subtracts layers of socks.

The exactness of small sounds consoles her:
a fly is awake filing on air.
The view comes in through the window
speaking in the sudden voice of a shy person.
She begins making a face for herself
out of a few squares of sky
fallen through the skylight to the floor.

Feet coming interrupt.
She turns the face she's working on
towards the slowly opening door.

THE HOLLOW QUIET

We exist marginally
on the thin air of this emptiness.
From my side of the room
wavering antennae reach
but don't make it.

My ears nervously record
the crackle of your voice revving up
to say, "I've got to go."
You drain out. Ebb away.

Into the vacuum the furniture flows back
and there in the watertight room
my hand turns the radio on like a faucet.

35

ONE OF THE MANY MANSIONS

Loose at the edge of the water she wanders,
a meanderer in white wild hair
walking into a wilderness
of thin things which sing.
She hears the trees in the park
having their own phantasies
and the grass whetting its blades.
Those who neither slumber nor sleep
pluck at her out of legends.
It's dark among the monuments,
and night has stretched out on the benches.

The cloth she's embalmed in
becomes frayed towards morning
but there are birds in the park
put there by God to clean bones
and as the night drifts away downriver
she is loosed into the beaks of gulls
flying higher than the phantasies of the trees
flying and turning in a blue bowl.

We are a flock of white balloons,
pale eyes, watchful around her.

LANDSCAPE

He's an earth lover, a land hugger,
a geophile, you might say.
The littlest mountain can turn him on
or the dingiest river.
I saw him smiling and crooning
at a puddle in a parking lot.
Old Reliable, that's Earth.
A person can always get a kick out of a tree
and it's no skin off the tree's teeth
if you love it and worry about its health.

So he walks through valleys of all colors
through shadows of differing thicknesses
and the earth stays trustworthy under his feet.
See him touching that boulder,
letting out love in a place that can't hit back?

OLD WOMAN STARTING TO SEW

She holds the steel sliver
at arm's length above soft cloth.
Draws thread taut between licked fingers
and jabs it at the needle's end:

    miss   miss   miss   miss

Oh the rich man too fat to pass through
wiggling away from heaven!
She wills him to be more tenuous,
straightens him again and focuses herself
in pinpoint attention on the feeler fibre
willing to lead the rest of him through.

    Oh the poor poor! and the unhappy rich!

THE DOUBLE SOLITUDE

1.

I am alone riding the river ferry.
The early water smokes in the frost.
Speaking to strangers
I come unfortified.

Whiskers of catfish
brush the bottom of the ferry
so that I leave it tickled and laughing.
Acorns patter on the roof of my car.

Down the clear passage to my center
comes the sound of the river flowing.

2.

There is a bag of green tomatoes
on the kitchen counter.
I am pickling them
and thinking about Survival.
The dog lies at my feet breathing
and asking to be stepped on
but I am nestbuilding carefully
with vinegar and green fruit.
Possibly we will have food for the winter.

I skirt the sleeping dog and hear
latches of doors
opening like kisses.

JACK-BUILT

This is the woman
this is the woman
this is the woman that Jack built.

This is the woman with velvet walls
with aquatints in her ochre halls

This is the woman who jangles dark
with doors unlocked and windows light
her beams and rafters bony white.
This is the woman that Jack built.

Over her roof
a luminous tree
flickers its leaves like a shadow play
and into her clean and empty rooms
the shadows brush like gentle brooms
sweeping a green and mossy haze
along her floors and over the sills
into the hall which the green light fills.

This is the woman
this is the woman
this is the woman that Jack built.

This is the child
who grew in the womb
of the mossy house with the marigold room.

This is the child with the startled eyes
who woke in the house
that shimmered and gleamed
who woke in the warmth
and grew in the green
who played in the shade
in the shade inside
inside of the woman that Jack built.

This is the child
of the leafy light
who patters in the listening leaves.
With windows open and door ajar
she echoes the rain like a sweet guitar
plucking at the mossy eaves
of the roof of the mother that Jack built.

This is the child who swarms with bees.
She was borne by the woman with sheltering eaves
who is green with moss and splashed with gilt
and she is the house that Jack built.

This is the girl
with the plumes of seed
who grew from the child
with the window panes
which look out on the grass of the waving plains.

This is the girl who grew from the child
who was born of the woman
who always hums
like the wind from the wild
when the banshee clock
strums in the house that Jack built.

And this is the wind
that toppled the tree
which crushed the roof
of the moss green mother.

This is the wind with the whispering roar
which sang through the grass
and smashed the door
of the mother who broke in a billowing tide
over the child who was still inside.

This is the wind in the streaming tree.
This is the rubble, this is the scree.
This was the woman that Jack built.

41

CROSSROADS

The sinuous cat at the cusp
crossing on purposeful paws
steps on dust
moved by cat laws.

Small neat hooves click
across chattering stones:
Donkey of Old Nick—
surefoot and steel bones.

Shawl blown out like a sail,
lame, in black and alone,
lurching down the trail
rocks an old crone.

Places of too many choices
crossroads are haunted they say
by wavering voices
calling "which way?"

Sharp hooves and soft paws
cross quick making no choice,
but the old black shoes pause,
she listens for a young voice.

Through wild thyme wind blows.
There are bells in the hills. Snow
on the mountains still. The stream flows.
Which way? Which way did he go?

OVER THE PASS

The old man hopped eagerly into the car
when I stopped to ask directions.
We two old sticks
drove up the mountain gabbling
each in his own language
about goats.

We stopped once to pick cherry branches
spangled with blossoming babies,
pink, they rode in his shaking hands
until he climbed out at his own house
smiled at the flowers and me
and said, "Addio."

I wound down the other side
of the Cretan mountain, my hand stretched out
to keep the babies from sliding off the seat.
"Is this old lady bursting into flower?"
I wondered, in low gear.
"How strong *is* spring?"

LEG

Such a shock I had
when I looked in the museum case
and saw your leg
drawn on the sherd beside the little pyxis.

How did an artist
in the fourth century B. C.
know what your leg would look like
jogging on the path around Fresh Pond?

POROS-GALATOS

Before dawn a man stood calling for a boat:
"Varka! Varka!"
through the hot dark.
Soon, nodding and bowing across the water
came the little taxi picked out in tinsel lights.

Now in white day these two towns
are strung together by a fleet of putting motors.
We are all, each of us, more
than three dimensional in the Greek light.

On my side of the water a surreal fisherman
stands by the lapping shadows.
In his hand a three-inch fish
like a silver votive, says
"Please, oh Pancreator,
take care of this little fish!"

The fisherman
looks down thoughtfully at his catch
and suddenly slips it back
between the trailing oars of the water taxis.

PENELOPE IN THREE SEASONS OF WAITING

first poem

Long fresh shadows
lie lightly on the beginning of day.
She breaks through the surface of sleep
her surface broken by reflections,
reassembles herself,
puts herself on like a dress.

Still new to waiting
she invents herself over and over
all day at the loom.
In the evening the nurse comes
with the child to her room.
They sit together unravelling and telling stories.
The nurse says islands are hallucinations of sailors, secrets
with moist clefts showing dark in the flanks of their hills,
she says they are imagined from ships too long at sea.

While they talk like this upstairs in the nursery
one or two young men, embarrassed,
sit on the back porch strumming their lyres,
still too shy to ask the cook for wine.

second poem

The sun explodes into a sky
bleached with heat.
Still as a statue the early fisherman
waits for news from the end of his line.

She wakes from the bursting plums of dreams
to a blanket of empty heat . . .
has tumbled all night through phantom hands
wakes from them sore and tender.

The men feasting below
echo in her body like shadows in water.
In the afternoons she bakes
like fish on a platter
in blander sauce.

Her son grows tall, his small deeds
buffeted by the feasters.
He talks of islands with water in his words
and knows: as long as the sea is there
it will be wandered on.

In the late cool her balcony
overhangs a promenading world
where people go in pairs
while she, the uncoupled watcher,
winds ravelled threads in skeins.

In the real dark she lies on her bed
holding herself together with her own hands.

third poem

At the end of summer in the hills
only the goats find anything to eat.
Dusty feet crunch on a dry earth.

She sits at her loom, professional at waiting.
Her hands and feet weave for her,
warehouses of linens.
Shoulders grown forward over the loom
can't be thrown back in welcome,
hope is shrunk to a small berry.
The habit of waiting obscures her like net,
dims her like tarnish on silver.
In her throat rise the bilious dregs of dreams.

She listens idly to islands
rising from some sub-aqueous place,
how they breathe with breath insubstantial as rumor.

The actual earth goes dry, goes fissured.
Dry leaves claw the walls,
wind scrapes the ground with them.
The rinds of the juiciest watermelons
have dried to dust-devils.
There are twisters twirling beyond the loom
into the moonscape of old age.

WALKING MUSIC

Climbing up to Chora in the noon hot days
the sea deep blue and the sun ablaze
the islands floating in a far off haze . . .
        Climbing up to Chora.

The wooden saddle on the donkey's back
like an armchair rocking up the stony track
and the land so dry   and her clothes so black . . .
        Riding up to Chora.

Waiting first on this foot and then on that
for a fleeting greeting as we overlap,
I stand beside the trail in my tourist hat . . .
        Going up to Chora.

Down below, a shepherd in the prickly spurge
shades his eyes to watch as our shadows merge.
In a momentary phantom separate lives converge
        As we go up to Chora.

EXCAVATION

We stand in a sleepy huddle
in the early wet light
on gritty unbroken ground.
In vaults below, the earth
hugs flint and bone
secretly away from the rain.

We make our plans in the rain:
where each of us will huddle
over a trowel, digging for the bone
we know must lie, light
and porous with its years in the earth.
We sniff the air and scuff the ground

like an impatient band of ground
squirrels prevented by fall rain
from digging nuts. Outside the huddle
of our raincoats the spring earth
smells promising. Bone
dry it would be dusty, the delight

of shovelling up the light
dust less than slicing the wet ground
aromatic from spring rain.
Hunters of flint and bone
without shelter, we huddle
on our marked off piece of earth.

Around our feet the earth
reaches its grasses into light.
Their roots explore the huddled
burial hidden in the ground,
tentacles feel each frail bone
while clumsy shovels glisten in the rain.

By eight the light has changed and now the rain
lifts from the ground. We break our huddle
to dissect the earth, to bare its broken bones.

PERSIA II

The Palace

A fluted column
lies in the sun in its loose stone skin
bleached golden.
We are stroking the glossy nostrils of bulls.

"Live 1000 years like a stone,"
said the sage in China and I'd try.
I'd try except for the interruptions:
The little boys with black polished eyes
the ticket collectors
the stone in my shoe .
Instead
I blow in time like a ragged banner.

The City

Invisible women pass all day in the street.
Wanting the same privilege,
I buy a length of black silk.
Shy Abdul, the concierge's nephew,
guides me to the old woman
who makes chadors for his mother.
She has blue eyes ,
crawls around me on lame knees,
snipping and pinning,
while Abdul stands in the courtyard,
averting his eyes,
until I am clothed in a fitting shadow.

The Garden

It was a surprise to come here and find winter,
no roses,
still fountains.
I look for two faces in the cold pools
and dislike the forgetful reflection.

If you came here again,
walking fast past the foolish water
to where I am sitting,
would your face be surprised
because you hadn't been expecting winter?

I huddle into my coat in the cold sun,
an old woman regretting a silly pilgrimage.

The Desert

Now at sunrise
twinkle-footed flocks pass
with young shepherds
whose eyes flash like knives.
A child in tinsel rags and wild red hair
drives water-buffalo to the river.

The desert flows past woolly and bleating.
I stand at the mudbrick gate
at the foot of my lazy shadow.

Behind me the courtyard shelters
one workable love
and a patch of green onions.

SUMMER DARK

Night is on duty
slung like a dark cape
over the houses.

With cool quiet fingers
she is working,
rearranging, opening up.

Like soft rain
she moistens the sleepers
spreading their petals.

she hovers over the dreamers,
holds them in her dark hands
out into the singing leaves.

IV

TRICYCLING THROUGH THE GREAT DEPRESSION

On her velocipede she learned
every wrinkle on the face of that zoo
where gray old men were washed up
among the animals.
It was the Depression for most people
but she had leather leggings which buttoned with a
    button hook.
She slept with them under her pillow.

Old men were stranded everywhere
on benches where she passed daily.
Even in the conservatory, their Florida,
they lolled under steamy bananas.
In warmer weather they picked cracker-jack boxes
out of trash barrels—looked inside them for sugar,
a disgusting thing to do, so she was told.

Four o'clock was feeding time in the lion house
and there, old men on benches warmed their hands
opposite the flickering cats.
When slabs of meat were thrown
they leaned a little forward
to watch eating.

She stood at the mouth high barrier
was told "Don't lick the railing!
          People have touched it!"
So she stood back between lions and old men
licking her ice cream cone. So little.
So obediently cold-hearted.

RETRIBUTION

" . . . to the tigers in the zoo
Madeline just said, 'Pooh! Pooh!' "
—Bemelmans

. . . except at night
except in bed
when over the sound
of cars of feet
of parents' voices
the terrible roars
come echoing out
of the resonant house
where the lions live
with a lazy keeper
who may forget
to lock the gates
which keep the cats
from slinking out
into the popcorn
littered dark
where in the night
they will recall
a girl like me.

From the zoo in the park
to the house where I lie
is only one
long   yellow   leap.

BUTTERFLY MAN

Forty floors up in the thinned noise
lives butterfly man, an old breeder
lepidopterist who holds

handfuls of perched light weights,
feeds them housegrown leaves
while their wings fan.

He watches each chrysalis
reach its fragile climax, burst its fruit
to dry in his box of bright fans.

They are gold and orange at sunrise
purple veined with gray at dusk, like the city.
At night his sleep is folded in their wings.

On a washed glass morning in winter
pressed for life time, he lets them out,
opens his southwest window wide.

Air rushes up and they go into it.
Warm currents from the street below
send the small wings on updrafts.

Bounced over the cold city
they fly a few wingbeats
until their small tropical constitutions

stop. And turning over and over they drop
slowly as leaves past the old face
like a wafer of light on the fortieth floor.

In his chest he feels the breathlong rise,
the lift, the faltering fall
of breath delicately fluttering to a close.

AIKIDO CLASS IN CALIFORNIA

They left off fighting like Americans
when the teacher came onto the mat.
One got kneed in the stomach and cried
but he's sitting now with the others
ready to make a small bow and begin.
They are dressed in the white of novices.

Their feet are neatly tucked
under their six-year-old bottoms.
They are Japanese-side-up
looking at the enormous teacher
in the wide black pants of an expert
who will show them violence danced.

In single file they circle the mat
practicing bonelessness.
First in line the teacher hurls himself
into an amazing roll and bounces upright
followed by eight speedy elastic rags
smiling because they love falling.

Feet in the proper position
the eight little boys learn throws in pairs.
One does the first easy wrist twist
while the other falls like laundry
without bones. They change places,
rubber puppies turning into Zen priests.

In a row by the wall
they duck the ferocious sword blows
aimed at their heads by the kindly teacher.
Practiced dodgers all of them;
not one breaks the cardboard sword
by allowing himself to be struck.

In the dressing room behind a curtain
the eight elastic little boys
put their bones back in
and their jeans back on.
They shamble back to their mothers
with their aikido costumes
bundled under their pointed elbows.
They're hungry for ice cream now
because it's a warm day in California
and Aikido is a Martial Art.

NIGHT SHIFT

The night mind squeezes and clucks,
strains and extrudes
long filaments of dream.
Words stenciled on silk
form and reform
coagulate in corners
slide down the silk to be runes.
Pennants stream from the sleeper,
moths hatch from her,
beat their wings slowly. Display.

She sinks for a moment
smothered in stuff,
tears a twist of silk from her throat,
sinks and rises
to bob on the run-off of her mind.
Gossamered over with spinnings
she reaches for the babies of sleep.

Yet when her eye opens
not a thread of silk
not a crumb of wing
lingers as record
or explanation.

TAKE-OFF

The take-off of every phoenix is awkward,
neck stretched out, wings flopping,
he scrabbles at the flames of disaster—
but once he's reached his altitude
he hovers on cool burnished wings.
over the burning years below.

How is it done, that kind of ballooning?
In theory I understand it well enough:
the stiffening sting of iodine,
rubbish in a ceremonial fire,
charcoaled stumps, wounds cauterized,
steel in a furnace.

But just now scuffling through charred scaffolding
among smashed feeders
and the smell of burnt feathers
scratching like chickens in the ashes,
most of us wonder, where's the updraft
to sail away on like a glowing cinder?

Some of them do it though.
Burnt somehow strong
they soar away easy
on well-tempered wings
carrying little rabbits of hope
in their talons.

IN THE LOCKED WARD LOUNGE
For my brother
1926-1975

No thanks, I don't want to play,
but thanks anyway.
You see this is me
walking around here
thinking
—though I may be Bertrand Russell.
Anyway I'm making a deal with God
which should make it O. K.
I'm always going to make myself very small,
never make any noise in the night,
not push in lines
or ask or take or want anything.
If I don't bump into them
nobody will notice me.
I might weasel through
exempt.
If things get dangerous
I can always hide in somebody else
like General Marshall
who wasn't afraid, and anyway
pretty soon I'll learn how to be
completely invisible . . .

see how I disappear
to just one pinpoint
where somebody keeps holding on to me
and pulling me back.
She says she's my mother
but if she lets go
I have it all figured out:
nobody will know I'm here
so I'll be what I'm trying for
i.e.
safe.

YELLOW DOG'S GOODBYE SONG

For my heart is full of honey
full as a big moon
and gold as fur.
The deepening snow is feather warm
and my heart is full of bright winter.

I am a piece broken out of the orange moon in summer
I sleep by a laid keel
I sleep in the pounding of hammers
I smell resin on my brother's hands
I watch him empty sawdust out of his shoes at night.

The ocean laps at my paws
and I hear the whisper of his boat
coming back at dawn through the fog.
My song is orange in the moonlight,
a golden pool in the corner of his silence.

I am many years in the good life of a dog
I am fur
I am ears
I am my brother's beginnings and inventions
and the biggest squash blossom in his garden.

While I sing
I am filling his tracks with pumpkin seeds
for my heart, ripe as a big moon, drops from the vine.

ARCHITECT

Donna Camilla chose the location
in the street below Santo Domingo
and became quickly ill with worry.
Shaken with chills in the afternoon
she lay all night in a fever of lists.
The little sisters brought her camomile
rubbed her with lotions
changed her sweaty linen for fresh.

A list blown into the garden
was raked up by Angelo
and taken to the priest to read:

    Kitchen fireplace at least three arches wide
        (room for broad-bottomed cooks)
    Refectory on the south
        (sunlight on food prevents diarrhea)
    Remember the importance of gardens
        to be subjects of praise
        to be courtyards to enclose us
    Washing. Done on Mondays by six gossiping sisters
        each requiring two tubs and a fall of light
        to direct her mind towards Heaven
    Squash gardens for Sister Francesca who wears
        boots under her habit in the muddy season
    Gardens with jasmine and hibiscus for the others
    Plants to remember:
        a pomegranate tree is important for teaching
                mythology
        pines grow quickly tall.
    Unglazed pots breathe better. Use them only.
        We will line our courtyards with geraniums.
    At least one fountain playing.
    One container for the spring.

There must be courtyards
　　to lead us toward Heaven by
　　　　their proportions
　　　　their flowers
　　　　their cloisters
　　Each courtyard must have its own clean latrine.

The priest reading the list laughed indulgently.
"Donna Camilla should have been a man.
Take it back to her Angelo."

Up on the hill in the temporary convent
Donna Camilla pulled herself back from delirium
to talk with the architect just arrived from Spain.
The sisters dressed her in her whitest
set two carved chairs in the shade of a mud-brick wall.

In the cooling afternoon
Don Romero sipped white wine
while she told him the requirements her lists held.

"One hundred sisters will come next year from Spain.
The convent you build them must be a step up towards Heaven.

Do you understand, Don Romero, how to use
　　Indian craftsmen and arches?
Can you build a latrine to the greater glory of God?"

He bowed to the lady and kissed her hand
　　and left on his horse in the dust.
She lay awake holding her rosary and a drawing of the
　　arches of paradise,
and she died in the dawn remembering the ovens she had
　　forgotten to order.

LONG DISTANCE

Our words huddle in anxious groups
pole to pole over mountains and gullies
helloing at each other
across long times and spaces.

How casually we used to look at each other
with voices shut up in our mouths.
Now our words teeter along the wire
but our eyes have gone silent forever.

You at your end, blind,
me at my end not able to see you.
You are in one dark
a long distance away,

I am in another kind here
holding this trickle of voice in my hand.

MAY FLOODS

Over here the raft swings,
slips down the current
through stumps and snags.

The great rivers in flood
spread over the cornfields
like brown cream.

Mississippi, Missouri, Illinois
sneaking under the houses.
All the land weeping into them.

In the Rock, the Red, the Fox
people are sitting
on the roofs of their cars, fishing.

A tangled string of barges
comes apart into islands.
The rivers are playing

funeral music for boys
back from drowning—tearful
in the shadows of the balcony.

Over there the Atlantic
is playing seagrass madrigals,
a rustling in the undertow

lightly ceremonial
while driftwood recorders
toot wistfully in the dunes.

As I look up from underwater
the face down faces trying to be happy
ripple down at me.

DAUGHTER

On some days my irritation is absolute.
Full of outsized words.
Nothing will assuage it.

I am peremptory and you do not care.
Oh the tininess of your eyes!
I put you to bed early with no light.

I am remembering programs
ruthlessly followed, remedial braces,
how often we disappointed each other.

I grow niggardly. I turn away.
I refuse to read you sad poems.
Oh Blacksmith Mother!

Now you lie with your anvil closed
while I, imperfect still,
plunge hissing into your slow death.

LITANY OF PRAIRIE FLOWERS

Indian paintbrush, blue-eyed grasses,
mountain mist and ladies' tresses.

My Lord we have made imperfect people out of clay.

Chicory and pink tick seed,
blazing star and joe pye weed.

Oh Lord, make me better in my own eyes.

Baneberry, blue vervain,
pickerel weed and wild fleabane.

Dear Lord, watch over me now I am old.

Milkwort, soapwort, gold poccoon,
blue-stemmed turkey foot in bloom.

My Lord, support me in dignity over the rim.

Virgin's bower and gentian hairy,
Queen Anne's lace and checkerberry.

Sweet Lord, notice and nurture me.

Lousewort, spurge and bergamot,
adder's tongue and touch-me-not.

Oh Lord, I am slipping out of your grasp.

foxglove, henbane, prairie dock,
bloodroot, meadow rue, hemlock.

Lord, you drop my fate, so careless, in my lap.

Sneezeweed, heal-all and boneset,
butter and eggs and bouncing bet.

It's the small things, Lord, that are hard to do.

JAPANESE PLATE

Ducking the blue willows
we walk right out of this city
into the narrow gorges.

Our hard shoes clack over an arched bridge
while rapids roar under. Two precise birds
fly up out of the reeds.

The path meanders up the mountain
to a brown ink teahouse
with a sketched bench.

We'll look down through interrupted mist
and in our eyes the last splinters of anger
will be dissolving. We'll pat each other's hands.
Our shoes will touch in brushstrokes of grass.

BREAK DANCERS IN SUBURBIA

Never before
between the colonial facade of the bank and
the antique shop with the cherry table in its window
has there been such
a sweet mix of people
dancing in the street or
a stomach-hopping four-year-old
admired as much as anybody
taking his non-agist turn, or
black and white boys
playing the slam-banging music
of 1984 to pace their own
invented use of the one smooth patch on
the white anglo-saxon sidewalk of
suburbia on a summer night in
the dark of the moon.

And watching,
just out of the movie across
the street, delighted bankers with
nodding and smiling golfing wives and
the serious steel gray lawyers of
the establishment laughing at
a child-invented future of
hardworking skillful inclusiveness
which—there between the Money Shop and
the Travel Bureau—turns out
to be an acceptable excellence after all.

CITY MORNING

An old woman leans in her window
like a soft boulder
feeling the day rise
lapping around its foundations.

The flesh of her arm swings
as she opens her window wider—
leans out farther to see more:
someone is carrying a ladder.

Down the street a man in a hardhat
is coming out of a manhole.
He talks to his supervisor
who sits in the doorway of a truck

making suggestions. Boys on skateboards
stop to rearrange themselves.
Grackles assemble in the budding trees
to discuss controversial subjects.

At the other end of the street
a lozenge of sun shines on a tulip
in a yard-square yard where, unemployed,
a cat is considering its plans.

Luminous open voices call out
while closed dark letters drop in slots.
One by one the docile cars
are leaving their night moorings.

The rising tide makes a cheerful bustle.
Yes, the night was long alone,
but now the morning she leans into
is short and warm.

BRINK

Please do come in.
Oops, mind the portcullis!
It droops a bit lately
since the lintel came loose.

Here, I'll hang your coat
on the new coathook in the guardroom,
the old headhooks fell out
when the bastion cracked.

This is the Great Hall.
Let me straighten the crooked ancestor
above the mantle. Bricks falling
disturb his balance.

Oof! Today the library is murky
with leather-binding dust.
And the collapsing cornices
scatter such plaster!

Now this is the salon.
Don't trip on that loose floorboard
by the Louis Quinze settee.
Isn't the view of the garden sweet?

Just beyond the little hedge—
well, you can't see it now,
the hedge needs clipping—is the sea.
Directly underneath us are the sands.

CALLING-PEOPLE

The president is walking in his sleep.
At the ends of his arms
air-flicking fingers thrum
dreaming of turning on a light.
Sleep, surrounded by switches,
is irridescent in the Dark House.
His sleepy hand fumbles and reaches,
cheerful. Numb. Near.

The rest of us in variegated costumes
wearing shoes with holes
cluster in the streets,
calling-people stepped into the darkness
where we dunk our lives
and leave our sleepy babies
with the future pulled up like a quilt.

We wake into the night
with our arms around a sentence:
"I am in a strange place—
that is to say, *the world*—
longing for home,"
while quietly
on the relentless soles of his slippers
the president is walking in our children's sleep.

BOY CARRYING A PEACE BANNER

If the world were made
of elderly relatives
at Christmastime
in the dark of the year

and if you could travel
tree to tree
plum pudding to plum pudding
reliably surprised

repeatedly delighted
by long-planned packages
of love-lit sweaters and
care-drenched socks,

and if you could keep on being
the Christmas child
trudging his December rounds
among detached

grandparents and those
deciduous uncles and aunts,
reaffirming for all, the worth
of joyfully beginning

next year's knitted wonder
one size larger in blue . . . then

you could probably induce
this flagging world to shamble on.

CHICKEN YARD AFTER THE FIRE

They scuffle through charred scaffolding
among feeders smashed splintery.
The smell of burnt feathers
hangs dreary over the cinders.
They are all singed ragged and burnt thirsty.

When they hear the noisy whirr of take-off
they dart their beady eyes around
a-flutter with hawk-fear
as the Leghorn cockerel, burnt somehow strong,
rises like an awkward phoenix
over the fence to the green meadow.
He stretches his neck
right out of the dust of disaster.
He flies.

Two frayed hens saying "Tsk! Tsk! Tsk!"
peek at him through the slats
of the chickenyard fence.
"The hutzpah of him!" they chatter to each other.
"No respect! No respect! No respect!"

RESEARCH

By noon
they are sitting in the library
looking up ancestors.
They are pulling out little drawers
in the department of genealogy.
They are making scratchy notes
on pictures of trees.

One goes home
to write letters
to his descendants,
carries himself
like a cup of water
brimming,
steps meticulously
not to spill himself
all over the sidewalk.

First he takes his clothes
to the corner cleaners
and cautiously brushes his thin hair.
Then, feeling balding and fragile,
he wonders
if he's the weakest link
in the whole
painstakingly
looked up
chain.

BALANCING BACK

Flying our birds like pennants
we step into thin green chiffon gowns
in an ancient commencement.
A procession of rare days
forms in the aisles of June.
Radiant after rain,
wet trees celebrate.
Wind rinses us and early sun
comes over us like silk.

The meadow is tossing its grass
wave after wave to the west.
We are marrying the future again,
boarding it like a boat.

THE OLD COUPLE

Their feet go barely
along the cool path.
They lay their towels
at the edge of the lake.

The counselor
says "stay close
to your buddy in the water."
It is night.

They are skinny dipping
in the slippery void
each believing
that the other can swim.

When the whistle blows,
when the treat is over,
they are not drowned,
though they may be sleepy.

They carry the wrong towels
home through the pines
then matter-of-factly
whisper each other to sleep.

OAK STREET

The bottoms of sleek condos
squat in the garden of the sooty
red building where I lived twice.
Everything is remade along Oak Street
except where the Newberry Library
holds open a big space
for stacks of familiar biography.

If I were famous too
someone would come right here
to take notes. Standing on this corner
they'd thrill to the presence of my past.
"Right under that building," the scholar
would write, "was the very courtyard
where her young father
pulled her sled in the snow.
Across the street
in the Piggly Wiggly Store
the grocer offered candy. 'Just one'
said her mother and she,
already unfaltering at three,
always chose the raspberry
with its chewy sour-sweet middle.
Is this significant?"

Peeking under the new buildings
this person doing research on me
would also discover me
pushing a gray wicker carriage,
the cat, Anna Pavlovna, asleep
heavy on the baby's feet.
"Her first child . . ." the scholar would jot,
recording the imprint of shadows.
But what about you and me
as the government began dismantling
the long absences of war?

Well, nobody else is writing this down
so I loiter along Oak Street
past the Newberry Library
recording myself on anything handy.
I erase the new buildings
estimate the distance to the corner,
and rubbing the sole of my shoe
on the bumpy old sidewalk
I write on my own stock
of invisible 3x5 cards:
"We stood here, anxious strangers,
that day when you. . . ."

I file these thin sheets of notes
in the perishable catalogue in my head
under "B" for babies, "O" for Oak Street,
and "U" for us. There isn't any
temperature control in these stacks,
but I'll look them up later and savor
the babies in transparent wicker,
the sweet raspberry taste of parents in snow,
and us, smelling of sweaty leather and new seams,
bounding out of our green convertible Ford coupe.

THE OUTSIDERS

I walk down the new street like anyone
doing a spring errand, buying a light
supper. The blossoms bow and bloom
casting to the left and to the right

little sweetnesses for the populace.
May wind laps at the trunks of trees,
inquisitively nuzzles my face.
I wrap myself in a transparent breeze.

I walk past a woman bent like a lover
to some grassy task in her green yard,
white hair lightly wisping over.
And such a pleasant hallooing is heard

where the schoolyard trampoline
catches and throws. On tot lot swings
small voices softly croon
and birds brush mothers with their wings.

Beside the corner grocery store
a stranger reaches out an empty hand,
asks me whispering for the time.
At first I do not understand,

I think that time is what he wants.
I look down at his bleeding feet
his bag of rags, his ragged pants . . .
Roped pre-school children pass us, neat

as laundry on a line. A tiny chain-gang
tired, hungry, for the moment, good.
Away from their opaque eyes, the stranger
twists, so they can't see him weep for food.

> Spring like a cloth on the ground, is spread
> with succulent sprigs and every juicy herb
> while all around its edges the outsiders
> watch and lean on their sticks at the curb.

ABOUT THE AUTHOR

Alice Ryerson has spent most of her life going to schools or working in them as parent, wife, teacher, psychologist, trustee, advisor, or student. She is the founder of the Ragdale Foundation, a place for writers and artists to work. Archaeology is her serious hobby. She has four children and seven grandchildren and lives with her husband, Albert Hayes, in Chicago. Her other books are *Excavation*, 1980, and *Matrimonial Picnic*, 1984.

ACKNOWLEDGMENTS

Grateful acknowledgment is made to the following publications in which some of these poems first appeared:

Beloit Poetry Journal, Confrontation, Dark Horse, Epos, Greenhouse, GRIST, Poetry, Prairie Schooner, Primavera, Sing Heavenly Muse, Spoon River Quarterly, Swallow's Tale, Women II, Yes, Our Bodies Ourselves (Boston Women's Health Book Collective), *Excavation* (Kelsey St. Press), and *Matrimonial Picnic.*

"Beyond the Candle" first appeared in *Poetry* (January 1943) and was copyrighted in that year by The Modern Poetry Association. It is reprinted here by permission of the editor.